The *1986 North American Waterfowl Management Plan* launched a new era in wildlife conservation, setting out a blueprint for developing public–private partnerships to conserve natural resources. Today, thousands of partners in our three nations have established a continental conservation legacy, one that is based on sound science and a landscape approach. Building on this foundation, the *1998 Update, Expanding the Vision,* envisions a North America where the needs of waterfowl—and indeed all wild species— are considered, as citizens participate in making decisions about the use of landscapes. We enthusiastically endorse this concept and encourage leadership by Plan partners in implementing this vision well into the next century.

Le *Plan nord-américain de gestion de la sauvagine de 1986* lançait une nouvelle ère en conservation de la faune, en établissant un plan directeur pour la création de partenariats publics-privés en vue de conserver les ressources naturelles. Aujourd'hui, des milliers de partenaires dans les trois pays ont établi un legs continental de conservation, fondé sur des données scientifiques solides et une approche axée sur les paysages. En bâtissant sur ce fondement, *la Mise à jour, 1998,* du document *Une vision élargie,* anticipe l'Amérique du Nord en tant que continent où les besoins de la sauvagine et de toutes les espèces sauvages sont pris en considération, étant donné la participation des citoyens aux prises de décision sur l'utilisation des paysages. C'est avec enthousiasme que nous appuyons ce concept et encourageons le leadership des partenaires du Plan dans la mise en œuvre de cette vision tout au cours du prochain siècle.

En *1986, el Plan de Manejo de Aves Acuáticas de Norteamérica* inició una nueva era en la conservación de la vida silvestre al establecer un esquema para la conservación de los recursos naturales, basado en el desarrollo de asociaciones entre el sector público y el privado. Hoy en día, miles de socios en nuestras tres naciones han establecido un legado de conservación a nivel continental, un legado con bases científicas y una aproximación al nivel de paisaje. Partiendo de este legado, *la actualización de 1998 del Plan Ampliando la visión* augura un futuro para Norteamérica en el que no solo se consideren las necesidades de las aves acuáticas sino de toda la vida silvestre, al mismo tiempo que los ciudadanos participen en la toma de decisiones sobre el uso de su entorno. Apoyamos con entusiasmo este concepto y alentamos el liderazgo de los socios del Plan para ir implementando esta visión dentro del próximo siglo.

Bruce Babbitt
Secretary of the Interior, United States

Julia Carabias Lillo
Minister of Environment, Natural Resources
and Fisheries, Mexico

Christine Stewart
Minister of the Environment, Canada

EXPANDING the VISION

1998
Update

NORTH AMERICAN

WATERFOWL

MANAGEMENT PLAN

North American Waterfowl
Management Plan

Plan nord-américain de
gestion de la sauvagine

Plan de Manejo de Aves
Acuáticas de Norteamérica

 U.S. Department of the Interior,
Fish and Wildlife Service

 SEMARNAP
Mexico

 Environment   Environnement
Canada   Canada

Canadian Wildlife   Service canadien
Service   de la faune

Contents

Figure

Tables

Map

Preface

The *North American Waterfowl Management Plan* (Plan), signed by Canada and the United States in 1986, laid out *A Strategy for Cooperation* in the conservation of waterfowl. It emphasized the importance of a partnership approach to conserve habitats important to waterfowl, to continually improve our scientific understanding of waterfowl populations and their interactions with habitats, and to periodically update the Plan.

In 1994, the Plan was updated and became a truly continental effort when Mexico joined Canada and the United States as a signatory. Although the principles and the waterfowl population goals in *Expanding the Commitment* remained the same as in the 1986 Plan, habitat objectives increased fourfold. The challenge was clear: more needed to be done on a broader scale.

The *1998 Update, Expanding the Vision*, builds on the legacy of the 1986 Plan and 1994 Update. The vision put forward here recognizes that the socioeconomic context for waterfowl conservation in North America is changing rapidly. Now more than ever, waterfowl conservation is linked to a wide range of social and economic policies and programs, and to other international wildlife conservation interests. The 1998 Update was developed in light of these changing circumstances and after extensive consultation. We hope that it will guide continental waterfowl conservation well into the next century.

It is also our hope that the Plan will remain a model for international conservation, and that its spirit of partnership and cooperation will inspire all people working to conserve North America's natural resources. To the many thousands of partners who have made the Plan a success, we salute your tireless efforts and commitment, and we look forward to your continued support. To the many others involved in conservation, we look forward to the opportunity of working together to conserve our nations' natural resources.

George Arsenault, Canada
Daniel M. Ashe, United States
Humberto Berlanga, Mexico
Arnold Boer, Canada
Jorge Correa, Mexico
Dick Elden, United States
Patricia Escalante, Mexico
Francisco Flores, Mexico
Eric Gustafson, Mexico

Thomas Hinz, United States
Eldridge "Red" Hunt, United States
Gerald McKeating, Canada
Bob McLean, Canada
Felipe Ramírez Ruíz, Mexico
Joshua Sandt, United States
Dennis Sherratt, Canada
David A. Smith, United States
Doug Stewart, Canada

The North American Waterfowl Management Plan Committee

Acknowledgements

The production of this 1998 Update document is due in large part to the very same spirit of tri-national partnership and cooperation embodied in the principles of the Plan itself. The Plan Committee gratefully acknowledges the time and support given by the following people, and we apologize to contributors we may have unintentionally omitted:

Pintails – U.S. Fish and Wildlife Service

Charles Baxter
Danielle Bridgett
Dee Butler
Ken Cox
Erika Delgado
Rod Fowler
Rich Goulden
Meredith Gutowski
Fred Johnson

Mark Koneff
Art Martell
Elisa Peresbarbosa
Barbara Robinson
Greg Thompson
Len Ugarenko
Steve Wendt
Ken Williams

"We have a chance to play a part in a landscape drama ... unfolding across the world's most richly blessed continent ... the opportunity to recreate the setting for the return of great flocks of wild waterfowl, of songbirds and marsh denizens of all kinds ...This requires vision ..."

Rich Goulden
1941 – 1997

Executive Summary

The *North American Waterfowl Management Plan* (Plan) is the most ambitious continental wildlife conservation initiative ever attempted. It seeks to restore waterfowl populations in Canada, the United States, and Mexico to the levels recorded during the 1970s—a benchmark decade for waterfowl. Several factors have combined in recent years to bring waterfowl populations remarkably close to this goal today. Tremendous achievements in habitat conservation—through the efforts of many Plan partners, new programs for wildlife habitat conservation, changes in agricultural conservation policies and programs, and exceptionally good hydrological conditions—have contributed to a striking rebound in most populations of ducks, geese, and swans.

Redhead — Ducks Unlimited Canada

While this response is encouraging, the enthusiasm of Plan partners is tempered by the realization that waterfowl populations are approaching Plan goals that were established for average environmental conditions rather than for the sustained excellent conditions of the past 4 or 5 years. The continuing growth of global population, the increasing demand for agricultural production, and the quest for an ever-increasing standard of living, combined with an inevitable return to average or below-average hydrological conditions, will likely depress waterfowl populations in the future. Thus, if waterfowl populations are to be sustained, conservation efforts must continually be adjusted.

The legacy established by the Plan in its first 12 years—implementing biologically based conservation across priority landscapes through innovative partnerships—has changed the approach to conservation as it pertains to all wildlife, not just waterfowl. Thousands of partners representing diverse interests in three countries have worked to conserve over 5 million acres of wetland ecosystems. Together, they have restored, protected, and improved habitats for migratory birds, amphibians, fish, mammals, and plants. Their efforts have helped to conserve North America's rich biological diversity, as well as provide environmental services such as water quality improvement and erosion control. In addition, the research and monitoring of specific populations conducted by the Plan's species joint venture partners has added to the knowledge base of these species and will improve their management.

> Thousands of partners representing diverse interests in three countries have worked to conserve over 5 million acres of wetland ecosystems.

In considering the history and future of waterfowl conservation within an ever-changing international context, the drafters of the 1986 Plan foresaw the need for periodic updates to keep the Plan responsive and relevant. It is in this spirit that the *North American Waterfowl Management Plan, 1998 Update, Expanding the Vision* reflects on the legacy established by the Plan and presents three visions to advance waterfowl conservation in the future:

- Plan partners enhance the capability of landscapes to support waterfowl and other wetland-associated species by ensuring that Plan implementation is guided by biologically based planning, which in turn is refined through ongoing evaluation.

  - Plan partners define the landscape conditions needed to sustain waterfowl and benefit other wetland-associated species, and participate in the development of conservation, economic, management, and social policies and programs that most affect the ecological health of these landscapes.
  - Plan partners collaborate with other conservation efforts, particularly migratory bird initiatives, and reach out to other sectors and communities to forge broader alliances in a collective search for sustainable uses of landscapes.

The challenges set forth in this 1998 Update form the basis for actions that will improve the status of North America's waterfowl, promote sustainable landscapes, and broaden partnerships on international, national, regional, and local levels.

Part 1 of this Update sets out a strategic direction for Plan partners to bring waterfowl conservation into the next century. After describing the Plan's conservation legacy, its accomplishments to date, and the changing international context in which the Plan must be implemented, Part 1 puts forth three visions for strengthening the Plan's biological foundation, moving toward landscape conservation, and broadening partnerships.

Part 2 outlines the Plan's population and habitat objectives for North America's ducks, geese, and swans. Finally, Part 3 gives an overview of the Plan's administration in Canada, the United States, and Mexico.

G. R. Harding

The challenges set forth in this 1998 Update form the basis for actions that will improve the status of North America's waterfowl, promote sustainable landscapes, and broaden partnerships.

PART 1

Strategic Direction

The North American Waterfowl Management Plan— A Conservation Legacy

For millennia, ducks, geese, and swans have migrated across North America's landscapes in an annual ritual that evokes a sense of wonder at the forces, mysterious yet consistent, that send millions of birds the length of a continent and back again. Yet among conservationists, the mystery of migration is accompanied by certain knowledge that waterfowl are dependent upon a complex and increasingly vulnerable chain of habitats extending across international borders. Underlying the spectacle of migration is a challenge of unprecedented proportions—the conservation of a migratory resource on a continental scale.

In 1986, the *North American Waterfowl Management Plan* responded to this challenge. It gave the wildlife conservation community the daunting task of coordinating and focusing the conservation programs of three nations to measurably increase continental populations of a highly mobile, shared migratory resource—waterfowl. First signed by Canada and the United States, the Plan was updated in 1994 with Mexico as a signatory. The 1986 Plan asked conservationists to develop coordinated site-specific habitat management programs and projects that would prompt population responses on a continental scale. It is this biological foundation that sets the Plan apart from most other conservation efforts of its time.

The Plan also recognized that land-use practices and policies affecting extensive areas across the continent would have to be altered. Conservation efforts would have to move beyond the limits of public natural resource lands to deal with whole landscapes, including private and common lands. Partners ventured beyond the security of long-established wildlife programs and relationships to embrace programs and policies that most directly affect the ecological health of landscapes—to benefit not only wildlife but people as well.

In addition, the Plan offered a platform from which waterfowl conservationists in both the public and private sectors could organize themselves into partnerships, called joint ventures, to accomplish this task. In 1994, Mexican regional partnerships, analogous to the U.S. and Canadian joint ventures, joined Plan efforts. This partnership concept would launch wetland habitat conservation into a new era by changing the way conservation is delivered.

Between 1986 and 1997, Plan partners invested over US$1.5 billion to secure, protect, restore, enhance, and manage wetlands and associated uplands in priority landscapes.

Between 1986 and 1997, Plan partners invested over US$1.5 billion to secure, protect, restore, enhance, and manage wetlands and associated uplands in priority landscapes; to conduct research and monitor specific waterfowl populations; and to provide environmental education and conservation planning with community involvement. Plan partners have worked within each country and internationally to influence agriculture, forestry, water, and trade policies that have indirectly affected a much larger portion of the continent's landscapes than have direct conservation projects alone.

Doug Ryan

Through the collective effort of Plan partners, the hopes of the Plan's original drafters have been transformed into a threefold conservation legacy, which is the foundation of the 1998 Update:

- The Plan's biological foundation links on-the-ground habitat management to quantified waterfowl population and habitat goals, objectives, and strategies that are both continental and regional in scope.
- The Plan has been a major force in moving the wildlife conservation community toward a landscape approach, one that integrates management and stewardship of public, private, and common lands.
- The Plan pioneered a partnership approach to conservation, which permeates all facets of Plan implementation.

Looking back to 1986, those associated with the Plan should be congratulated for their record of exceptional contributions to habitat and species conservation. The Plan's vision of biologically-driven, science-based partnerships focused on landscape-level change has become a reality.

The Changing Context of Waterfowl Conservation

For the past 100 years, waterfowl conservation in North America has adapted to changing environmental, economic, social, and political forces. Now, as Plan partners consider the future of waterfowl conservation in this 1998 Update—and work ever more closely with each other in the three countries—they must respond to continuing fundamental shifts in the international context that shaped and directed the drafting of the original Plan in 1986.

Ducks Unlimited Canada

Evolution of Waterfowl Conservation in North America

The institutional framework for international cooperation in conserving North America's migratory birds was established early in this century. In 1916, Canada and the United States signed a treaty for the conservation of migratory birds, and in 1936 the United States and Mexico signed a similar convention. By the 1980s, a long tradition of international cooperation in waterfowl population surveys and harvest management was in place. Population data confirmed that accelerated conversion and degradation of habitat caused by human activities, and an extended period of below-normal precipitation on mid-continent prairie landscapes, had led to a series of record-low populations of most duck species. The need was clear: international cooperation in harvest management must be extended to include habitat conservation. This need was answered by the Plan in 1986 and by its Update in 1994.

As a result, Canada, the United States, and Mexico now share the responsibility and costs of implementing conservation under the Plan. But they also share the significant benefits that flow to many economic sectors as a result of healthy North American migratory bird populations. More than 60 million people who watch migratory birds and 3.2 million who hunt waterfowl generate over US$20 billion annually in economic activity in North America.

While the Plan's focus is on the conservation of waterfowl habitat, the benefits resulting from the efforts of Plan partners extend well beyond migratory bird conservation. Plan partners are increasingly modifying project designs to capture benefits for other wildlife, including endangered species, and for hydrology and water-quality improvement.

> More than 60 million people who watch migratory birds and 3.2 million who hunt waterfowl generate over US$20 billion annually in economic activity in North America.

Current Continental Context of the 1998 Update

Canada, the United States, and Mexico also participate in other alliances in conservation and trade that directly affect waterfowl conservation, creating obligations, opportunities, and challenges for Plan partners. These include the Convention on Wetlands of International Importance (Ramsar, Iran, 1971), the 1992 Convention on

Biological Diversity, the 1992 North American Free Trade Agreement and the parallel North American Agreement on Environmental Cooperation, and the Tri-Lateral Committee for the Conservation and Management of Wildlife and Ecosystems. While each of these initiatives reflects an increasing awareness of the economic and environmental benefits of international cooperation, together they form an increasingly complex and diverse institutional context within which the Plan must be implemented.

An important element of these alliances is the integration of Mexico as a full partner in the conservation of North America's biological wealth. In Canada and the United States, despite relatively elaborate public and private conservation programs, the conservation movement has developed and matured largely outside of mainstream socioeconomic policy. Only within the past decade, through the advancement of the concept of sustainable development, has convergence begun. In contrast, Mexico is developing its socioeconomic and conservation policies and infrastructure more in tandem, guided by an explicit recognition of the implications of convergence of these policies to delivery of the Plan and to biodiversity conservation in general.

Another element critical to the success of these initiatives is the role of the continent's Aboriginal, Native American, indigenous, and local communities, for which migratory birds have cultural and dietary importance. Internationally, this is now acknowledged through the 1995 and 1997 amendments to the Migratory Bird Conventions, which recognize the importance of the traditional subsistence harvest of waterfowl. Nationally, the role of Aboriginal, Native American, indigenous, and local communities in the management of migratory birds and in the stewardship of vast areas of migratory bird habitat will continue to evolve. In Mexico, for example, where almost all of the land is either private or common land, it is especially important that residents play an active role for conservation to be effective.

Ultimately, the success of the Plan will depend on effective partnerships among all sectors of society that have a role in waterfowl conservation.

Other Migratory Bird Initiatives

In 1986, waterfowl conservation on an international level was largely synonymous with migratory bird conservation since formal international partnerships aimed at non-game migratory birds were only beginning to emerge. The Western Hemisphere Shorebird Reserve Network was less than one year old, and it would be almost five years before Partners In Flight would begin to address more than 700 other species of non-game migratory birds. More recently, a coalition of interested partners has begun to consider a conservation plan for colonial waterbirds.

Inspired by the success of the Plan, these international efforts are now engaged in conservation planning on a continental scale, thus broadening the scope and vitality of migratory bird conservation in North America. In addition, a broad coalition of government, non-government organizations, and academia is considering how best to coordinate and integrate these bird conservation plans. The Commission on Environmental Cooperation is facilitating this effort through the North American Bird Conservation Initiative.

The U.S. government provided an incentive for Canada, the United States, and Mexico to accelerate cooperative migratory bird conservation efforts with passage of the North American Wetlands Conservation Act in 1989. The Act's grant program encourages and supports partnerships to conserve wetland ecosystems and the waterfowl, other migratory birds, fish, and wildlife that depend upon these habitats in the three countries.

John Heinz

Trends

Changes in the international context—global and continental—will continue to present challenges to Plan partners in managing landscapes important to waterfowl and other migratory birds and wildlife.

Demographic patterns are undergoing fundamental shifts. For the first time in history, the majority of humans now live in urban areas. In Canada and the United States, the number of absentee landowners and corporate agricultural operations is increasing, while the number of family farms is decreasing. In some parts of central and northern Mexico, a similar resettlement has begun. One result of this shift is the loss of first-hand understanding and experience of many ecological processes and on-the-ground conservation practices. As people become disconnected from the land and are increasingly influenced by urban lifestyles, their appreciation for and understanding of soil, water, and wildlife issues and practices declines.

Since the early 1980s, the number of waterfowl hunters in Canada and the United States has declined significantly. However, the number of people active in other forms of outdoor recreation, such as bird watching, has grown rapidly. Hunters have been long-standing, vocal supporters of conservation, and have contributed substantially to habitat conservation projects. Others who are equally concerned about and benefit from conservation must be encouraged to contribute as hunters have. This will help to ensure that conservation efforts are sustained over time and that the associated costs are more fairly distributed.

The increased demand for grain production caused by continued growth in the world's population will create incentives to convert more grassland and wetland areas for intensive farming. Additional pressures to increase grain production in North America could reduce both broad support for, and incentives for farmers to participate in, several programs that have been critical to the Plan's success to date. These include agricultural conservation programs such as the Conservation Reserve Program and Wetlands Reserve Program in the United States; the Prairie CARE (Conservation of Agriculture, Resources, and the Environment) and Ontario CARE programs in the United States and Canada; and natural resources programs such as the System of Units for Conservation Management and Sustainable Use of Wildlife and the Natural Protected Areas System in Mexico.

Changes in the international context—global and continental— will continue to present challenges to Plan partners in managing landscapes important to waterfowl and other migratory birds and wildlife.

On the other hand, through deliberations of the World Trade Organization, under the auspices of the General Agreement on Tariffs and Trade, subsidies for commodity production are being reduced or eliminated. Plan partners hope that as land-use decisions respond to the demands of the marketplace, practices and policies will evolve toward those that are sustainable and that allow for wildlife conservation in agricultural landscapes.

Roger Bryan

Finally, the issue of global climate change has spurred considerable debate on the extent to which meteorological trends are influenced by human activity. Regardless of the cause of these trends, minor changes in climate may have profound effects on wetland ecosystems, particularly those already stressed by degradation. Adaptive conservation strategies are needed to anticipate and address changes.

The drafters of the 1986 Plan foresaw the need for periodic updates to keep the Plan responsive and relevant. It is in this spirit that the 1998 Update reflects on the legacy established by the Plan and presents a vision for the future, carrying the Plan forward until the next Update in 2003.

Expanding the Vision

Strengthening the Biological Foundation

The Vision

Plan partners enhance the capability of landscapes to support waterfowl and other wetland-associated species by ensuring that Plan implementation is guided by biologically based planning, which in turn is refined through ongoing evaluation.

Ducks Unlimited Canada

I f the Plan is to achieve its goal of restoring and maintaining waterfowl populations in the face of current demographic, economic, and environmental trends, its biological foundation must be strengthened. This biological foundation logically links the Plan's continental population goals to its regional conservation strategies and, therefore, depends upon knowledge of how landscape conditions affect waterfowl abundance.

The Plan's biological foundation can be strengthened through a systematic process of strategic planning, implementation, and evaluation, where:

- *planning* relies on management objectives and the anticipated effects of management actions to evaluate alternative conservation strategies;
- *implementation* proceeds in accordance with the preferred conservation strategy, recognizing constraints on conservation actions and limits to biological understanding; and
- *evaluation* measures progress toward management objectives and provides a basis for refined strategies in future planning efforts.

In this context, the justification for biological planning is to ensure successful conservation strategies, while the rationale for evaluation is to improve the effectiveness of that planning.

Actions that will advance the strengthening of the Plan's biological foundation are described below.

> The Plan's biological foundation can be strengthened through a systematic process of strategic planning, implementation, and evaluation.

Develop measurable, scale-specific management objectives that provide the basis for planning and evaluation

The continental population goals first established in 1986 provide the Plan with its ultimate measures of performance. As useful as continental population goals are, however, they are inadequate for planning and evaluating management activities at regional or local scales. Therefore, the objectives that Plan partners identify should be both measurable and appropriate to the geographic scale under consideration. These objectives might involve regional population targets or reflect desired levels of reproduction and survival. Whatever form they take, the relationships among objectives at the various geographic scales of interest should always be explicit and logical.

Enhance planning and evaluation by expanding monitoring and assessment capabilities

The monitoring and assessment programs used to guide waterfowl management in North America are among the best such programs in the world. However, mechanisms to monitor environmental conditions and the effects of landscape changes on waterfowl are not well developed. These monitoring and assessment capabilities remain beyond the reach of many Plan partners because available resources have been insufficient. Therefore, Plan partners should endeavor to develop funding sources for these programs in a fashion that enhances, rather than detracts from, delivery of the Plan.

Enhance Plan delivery by drawing upon biological information

Plan partners are encouraged to tighten their conservation focus by identifying regional landscapes, watersheds, or ecosystems most critical to meeting Plan goals, and by determining and documenting major limiting factors to waterfowl abundance in those areas. In doing so, Plan partners should ensure that conservation planning complements and is integrated with other wildlife and natural resource interests as much as possible.

Design and carry out evaluations in association with conservation strategies

Designing and carrying out evaluations in tandem with regional and local conservation strategies can be an extremely effective approach for enhancing future planning and implementation. Management actions that improve understanding of waterfowl biology and habitat ecology, taken with due regard to the needs, perspectives, and constraints of Plan partners, should be an integral feature of this approach.

Success in strengthening the Plan's biological foundation can be measured by the ability and willingness of Plan partners to deliver conservation strategies that are based on a systematic process of strategic planning, implementation, and evaluation. Ultimately, however, success can be measured by the extent to which there is agreement between the expected and realized consequences of conservation strategies. Such agreement would reflect a sound understanding of how landscape conditions affect waterfowl abundance.

As waterfowl conservationists strengthen the Plan's biological foundation, they will be better able to understand and predict the likely biological consequences of specific landscape conservation actions. Therefore, long-term solutions must incorporate landscape factors that influence waterfowl use of local habitats, and ultimately must account for their influence in evaluating the biological impacts of proposed conservation actions. In this way, a commitment to improving the Plan's biological foundation leads directly to a landscape approach to Plan delivery.

As waterfowl conservationists strengthen the Plan's biological foundation, they will be better able to understand and predict the likely biological consequences of specific landscape conservation actions.

Mallards — SEMARNAP

Toward Landscape Conservation

The Vision

Plan partners define the landscape conditions needed to sustain waterfowl and benefit other wetland-associated species, and participate in the development of conservation, economic, management, and social policies and programs that most affect the ecological health of these landscapes.

E ffective delivery of the Plan requires an understanding of the landscape context in which conservation efforts are directed. While public lands provide critical habitat and refuge for waterfowl and other migratory birds, most areas used by these species are on landscapes also used to produce economic returns—working landscapes that sustain communities through such activities as agriculture, mining, fishing, and forestry. Across the continent, these important landscapes include wetlands, aquatic systems, grasslands, forests, riparian areas, and nearshore seascapes.

A landscape approach to habitat management seeks to balance conservation and socioeconomic objectives within a region. To achieve Plan population goals, a myriad of habitats must be conserved, most of which exist in working landscapes. The interests of the people who share these landscapes with wildlife must be considered if Plan goals are to be achieved. The Plan provides the institutional framework for all conservationists to work with these interests to achieve mutual benefits across the continent's landscapes.

Actions that will advance a landscape approach to conservation are described below.

U.S. Fish and Wildlife Service

A landscape approach to habitat management seeks to balance conservation and socioeconomic objectives within a region.

Define and implement waterfowl conservation in a landscape context

Plan partners should strive to clearly place waterfowl conservation as a legitimate and necessary component of sustainable landscapes. Expressing habitat objectives in terms of specific and measurable goals for landscapes, and instituting systems to monitor habitats, will provide a sound rationale for establishing the direction, magnitude, and urgency of specific waterfowl conservation actions within particular landscapes.

Expand habitat conservation coordination across landscapes with other wildlife initiatives

Plan partners should improve habitat conservation coordination with other wildlife initiatives, including those directed at other migratory birds, endangered species, fisheries, and biodiversity. This will create mutual benefits in defining the direction, magnitude, and urgency of conservation actions within landscapes and in making wildlife conservation relevant in the broader context.

Seek landscape solutions that benefit waterfowl conservation goals and other needs

Plan partners should renew efforts to influence non-wildlife programs and policies that affect the health of the landscapes upon which waterfowl depend. In particular, agriculture, forestry, water, and trade policies should be influenced to improve habitats for waterfowl and other migratory birds. Such efforts should highlight the capabilities of these sectors to help meet waterfowl goals and the capabilities of conservation actions under the Plan to help meet the objectives of these other sectors.

> Long-term success of the Plan will depend on the commitment of local communities to the concept of stewardship, which includes planning, implementation, and caretaking.

Implement community-based projects within a landscape context

Long-term success of the Plan will depend on the commitment of local communities to the concept of stewardship, which includes planning, implementation, and caretaking. Therefore, waterfowl conservation should, wherever possible, be implemented through community-based projects and programs. This will promote landscapes capable of sustaining both economic progress and ecological process, and will ultimately secure the future for waterfowl. Such an approach will identify common concerns, goals, and conservation incentives and disincentives; emphasize education and outreach; and formulate conservation approaches that lead to mutually beneficial results.

As landscapes critical to waterfowl are managed by a wide range of diverging interests, and because conserving these landscapes is too big a job for any one organization or agency, implementing a landscape approach to conservation must be done through partnerships that involve land managers and other partners. By expanding the partnerships that have been a hallmark of the Plan, more skills, more resources, and more energy can be brought to bear on conservation actions. In this way, a commitment to focusing on landscapes leads directly to a partnership approach to Plan delivery.

Ducks Unlimited Canada

Broadening the Scope of Partnerships

The Vision
Plan partners collaborate with other conservation efforts, particularly migratory bird initiatives, and reach out to other sectors and communities to forge broader alliances in a collective search for sustainable uses of landscapes.

The drafters of the 1986 Plan realized that restoring waterfowl populations would require more than federal intervention on federal lands with federal dollars. In fact, federal approval of the 1986 Plan was predicated on the clear acknowledgement that fiscal responsibility for its implementation did not lie solely with the federal governments. Waterfowl conservation may have had its roots in international treaties, but the resources to support it would have to come from the private, state, provincial, and federal sectors.

What began as an acknowledgement of fiscal realities became the foundation and motivation for an innovative way of doing business: public–private partnerships. International Plan implementation was initiated when U.S. conservation organizations began matching funds from state wildlife agencies and facilitating the transfer of monies across an international border, to be further matched and expended by private, provincial, and federal entities within Canada, and eventually Mexico.

This new approach to conservation helped stimulate passage of the North American Wetlands Conservation Act of 1989, which created a funding mechanism for wetlands projects conducted under the Plan. Today, the concepts of pooling, matching, and sharing resources have been replicated so often by Plan partners that the business of waterfowl conservation has undergone a fundamental and enduring change.

The success of the Plan has hinged on the ability of diverse interests to create and sustain new relationships flexible enough to invent new ways of delivering waterfowl conservation. This legacy is one of the Plan's most important contributions to natural resources conservation. In some regions, these partnerships have expanded beyond waterfowl to include soil and water conservationists, land and water resource development interests, and, most importantly, private and community landowners.

Actions that will advance the broadening of partnerships are described below.

The success of the Plan has hinged on the ability of diverse interests to create and sustain new relationships flexible enough to invent new ways of delivering waterfowl conservation.

Broaden partnerships with other migratory bird conservation initiatives
The challenge of a landscape approach to conservation is not unique to waterfowl conservationists. As other migratory bird initiatives or conservation efforts face similar challenges, the need and opportunities for cooperation will grow. Plan partners should seek out and establish relationships with partners of those initiatives having common goals. Specifically, these partnerships should focus on the coordination of biological planning, implementation of habitat conservation, and cooperation in long-term habitat and population monitoring programs.

Significant local and regional waterfowl habitats exist outside established joint venture/ regional partnership areas or designated Waterfowl Habitat Areas of Major Concern. Often, these landscapes are imbedded within a physiographic region of concern to other migratory bird initiatives. Plan partners should seek to participate in the development of other landscape-level, migratory bird conservation plans to ensure that waterfowl needs are considered. Likewise, representatives of other migratory bird initiatives may be invited to participate in planning efforts to identify habitat needs of those species that should be considered by Plan partners. Eventually, a joint venture/regional partnership may be affiliated with more than one of these initiatives.

Seek partnerships with other economic sectors to meet common goals

Wherever cooperation can address resource problems of mutual concern, Plan partners should join partnerships in sectors other than wildlife to influence programs and policies that can contribute to the Plan's goals and jointly improve the environment's overall health. The Plan's initial focus on establishing partnerships with private and community landowners, the soil and water conservation community, and land and water resource development interests has not changed, and should be further emphasized.

Support and encourage conservation partnerships with communities

The Plan's vision of sustaining waterfowl populations within working landscapes can best be met by forming partnerships with communities to address their many conservation, social, and economic needs. To plan, deliver, and safeguard habitat conservation, Plan partnerships should include community leaders, Aboriginal, Native American, indigenous and local communities, and subsistence users in addition to conservation interests. Rural communities will also be pivotal in the conservation of waterfowl.

The figure below shows a conceptual model of the opportunities for cooperative conservation among separate and distinct conservation initiatives that have overlapping interests on landscapes. Each initiative maintains its own identity while cooperating with others in planning, implementation, or evaluation activities, and on regional, national, or international geographic scales. This model applies equally to migratory bird conservation initiatives and other science-based conservation efforts. It uses a landscape approach based on the needs of partners, providing joint ventures/regional partnerships and nations flexibility in implementing the Plan.

Figure
Model for cooperative habitat conservation

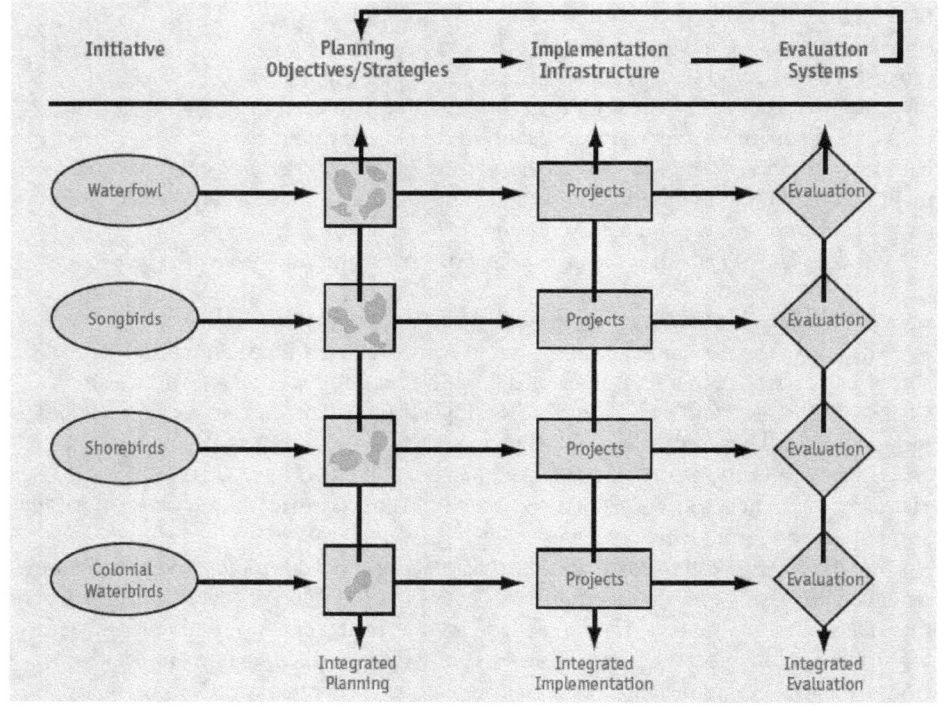

Summary

The Challenges

Implementing the Plan successfully depends on the interest, commitment, expertise, and resources of volunteer partners. These partners face challenges in:

- continuing the cooperation among three nations with different cultures and languages;
- maintaining current partners and enlisting new ones;
- expanding the capability to monitor habitats and populations and to evaluate management practices and programs;
- continuing and expanding species-specific research and monitoring;
- continuing and expanding community education and involvement in conservation planning;
- obtaining future legislative and administrative support to implement the Plan;
- developing partnerships with other migratory bird efforts;
- developing and improving partnerships with other conservation efforts;
- influencing policies and programs that direct agriculture, forestry, and trade toward waterfowl and wetlands conservation;
- defining landscapes that will sustain waterfowl concomitantly with other interests;
- evolving and adapting to changing conditions to ensure that Plan goals are achieved; and
- avoiding complacency after a job well done.

Snow Geese — Credit Unknown

The Visions

The 1998 Update offers three visions that build upon the Plan's legacy.

Plan partners enhance the capability of landscapes to support waterfowl and other wetland-associated species by ensuring that Plan implementation is guided by biologically based planning, which in turn is refined through ongoing evaluation.

Plan partners are asked to:

- develop measurable, scale-specific management objectives that provide the basis for planning and evaluation;
- enhance planning and evaluation by expanding monitoring and assessment capabilities;
- enhance Plan delivery by drawing upon biological information; and
- design and carry out evaluations in association with conservation strategies.

Plan partners define the landscape conditions needed to sustain waterfowl and benefit other wetland-associated species, and participate in the development of conservation, economic, management, and social policies and programs that most affect the ecological health of these landscapes.

Partners are asked to:
- define and implement waterfowl conservation in a landscape context;
- expand habitat conservation coordination across landscapes with other wildlife initiatives;
- seek landscape solutions that benefit waterfowl conservation goals and other needs; and
- implement community-based projects within a landscape context.

Plan partners collaborate with other conservation efforts, particularly migratory bird initiatives, and reach out to other sectors and communities to forge broader alliances in a collective search for sustainable uses of landscapes.

Partners are asked to:
- broaden partnerships with other migratory bird conservation initiatives;
- seek partnerships with other economic sectors to meet common goals; and
- support and encourage conservation partnerships with communities.

PART 2

Population Objectives and Status of North American Waterfowl

Population Objectives

North America has 43 species of ducks, geese, and swans that typically depend on habitats in two or more countries to complete portions of their life cycles. Population objectives have been established for most North American waterfowl and are described below. Specific objectives for other wildlife species inhabiting wetlands may be included in joint venture/regional partnership implementation plans established under the Plan.

Although ducks, geese, and swans are not isolated components of wetland communities, they represent one of the best documented sources of long-term data associated with wetlands. There is no other comparable inventory of fauna or flora associated with wetlands.

The factors adversely affecting waterfowl in North America are eroding the biological diversity of entire ecosystems. Similarly, Plan population objectives cannot be achieved without restoring ecosystems upon which waterfowl depend.

Specific Waterfowl Management Issues

In addition to applying the Strategic Direction in Part 1, Plan partners should address specific waterfowl concerns and problems to advance the Plan's population objectives and vision of a strengthened biological foundation.

For example, available data point to declines in many of the 15 species of North American sea ducks. Three of these species are classified as threatened or endangered in the United States or Canada. To recover and safeguard these species, coordinated research and monitoring actions to develop habitat management and policy recommendations are urgently needed. A sea duck joint venture is conditionally endorsed by interested agencies and organizations as the most appropriate mechanism to facilitate international coordination and cooperation for addressing this resource issue.

Several other species of ducks, notably northern pintail, have not responded to habitat improvements and seemingly excellent habitat conditions. Additional efforts are needed to better understand the factors that have limited the recovery of these species and populations, and to develop conservation actions to achieve population objectives. In addition, some goose populations, such as Atlantic Flyway Canada geese, remain well below Plan goals. Efforts should continue in the management of this and other below-target goose populations.

On the other hand, some Arctic nesting goose populations have reached levels well in excess of Plan goals, due in part to abundant crop forage on wintering grounds. This has created serious problems, including crop and habitat degradation. Expanding Arctic goose breeding colonies have severely degraded some tundra nesting and brood-rearing areas. The Arctic Goose Joint Venture should continue working with others to develop solutions to this waterfowl management problem.

Temperate zone nesting populations of Canada geese have also increased dramatically in some regions. Agricultural depredation, reduced water quality, and such problems as fecal accumulation in public areas are concerns in many regions. While partnerships involving farmers, hunters, conservationists, and public agencies have been addressing this issue in some regions, the scope of efforts should be expanded.

Conservation efforts under the Plan have focused primarily on migratory waterfowl. In order to address all of North America's waterfowl, however, the Plan's scope should be broadened to include national and regional planning for and management of endemic or non-migratory waterfowl species such as whistling ducks and masked ducks.

Disease has led to significant waterfowl mortality in certain regions of North America and continues to be a concern among waterfowl conservationists. Regional partnerships should continue to improve understanding of the causes of waterfowl diseases, such as botulism and fowl cholera. They should also continue to develop actions to reduce and control the effect of diseases where the intensity and frequency of occurrence threatens species or populations.

In some portions of Mid-continent breeding habitats, excessive predation is seriously affecting populations of some waterfowl and other ground-nesting birds. More effective predation management strategies may be considered in these situations within an overall landscape approach to management.

Several other species of ducks, notably northern pintail, have not responded to habitat improvements and seemingly excellent habitat conditions.

Pintails — Ducks Unlimited Canada

Duck Population Objectives

The abundance of ducks in North America from 1970 to 1979 is the baseline reference for duck population objectives under the Plan (Table 1). The 1986 Plan contended that duck numbers during the decade of the 1970s, with the exception of a few species, generally met the needs of all users. This number of ducks and the amount of habitat required to support them throughout their annual cycle determined the major objectives of the Plan. Thus, information from the 1970s supported the overall objectives of 62 million breeding ducks and a fall flight of 100 million birds under average environmental conditions—that is, average weather conditions in the Mid-continent Region.

Goals

Maintain the current diversity of duck species throughout North America and achieve a continental breeding population of 62 million ducks (mid-continent population of 39 million) during years with average environmental conditions, which would support a fall flight of 100 million

Reach or exceed mid-continent population goals for the 10 individual species in Table 2

Attain a black duck mid-winter population index of 385,000[a]

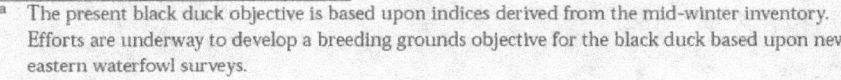

---

[a] The present black duck objective is based upon indices derived from the mid-winter inventory. Efforts are underway to develop a breeding grounds objective for the black duck based upon new eastern waterfowl surveys.

Table 1

Average duck population estimates[a] for North America, 1970–1979 (1,000s of ducks)

Species	Continental	Mid-continent
DABBLING DUCKS		
Mallard	11,000	8,199
Northern pintail	7,000	5,596
Black duck	1,400	30
Mottled duck	480	not applicable
Gadwall	2,000	1,518
American wigeon	3,500	2,974
Green-winged teal	3,000	1,858
Blue-winged and cinnamon teal	6,000	4,653
Northern shoveler	2,000	1,990
Wood duck	3,000	not applicable
Muscovy duck	30	not applicable
Fulvous and black-bellied whistling ducks	136	not applicable
DIVING DUCKS		
Redhead	900	639
Canvasback	600	542
Lesser and greater scaup	8,000	6,302
Ring-necked duck	1,000	506
Ruddy duck	700	352
Masked duck	6	not applicable
SEA DUCKS[b]		
Harlequin	200	not applicable
Oldsquaw	2,700	428
King, common, Steller's, and spectacled eider	2,500	23
Black, white-winged, and surf scoter	2,000	1,476
Bufflehead	1,000	724
Common and Barrow's Goldeneye	1,500	481
Hooded, red-breasted, and common merganser	1,500	403
TOTAL DUCKS	**62,152**	**38,694**

a Mid-continent estimates were derived from the Waterfowl Breeding Population and Habitat Survey, strata 1–18, 20–50, and 75–77. Continental estimates include the mid-continent estimates as well as rough estimates of populations outside the Mid-continent based on winter inventories and expert opinion. New surveys have been established in breeding areas in the northeast United States and eastern Canada, which should be useful in refining estimates and goals for certain species in the future.

b Harlequin ducks in eastern Canada and spectacled and Steller's eiders have been classified as endangered or threatened.

Table 2

Breeding duck population status, trends, and goals for the 10 most common species in the Mid-continent Region[a] (1,000s of ducks)

Species and Population	1985 Status	1998 Status	Recent Trend (1986-1998)	Population Goals
Mallard	4,961	9,640	Increasing	8,200
Northern pintail	2,515	2,521	No trend	5,600
Gadwall	1,303	3,742	Increasing	1,500
American wigeon	2,051	2,858	Increasing	3,000
Green-winged teal	1,475	2,087	Increasing	1,900
Blue-winged and cinnamon teal	3,502	6,399	Increasing	4,700
Northern shoveler	1,702	3,183	Increasing	2,000
Redhead	578	1,005	Increasing	640
Canvasback	376	686	Increasing	540
Lesser and greater scaup	5,098	3,472	Decreasing	6,300

a   Survey strata 1–18, 20–50, and 75–77 of the Waterfowl Breeding Population and Habitat Survey

Table 2 presents the Plan's duck population objectives and current status of duck breeding populations in the Mid-continent Region, where the majority of North American ducks breed. Of the 10 most common species breeding in the prairies, 8 have increasing trends for 1986–1998, the period of Plan implementation. Only scaup exhibited a decreasing trend, and are now 45 percent below the Plan population objective. Pintail numbers, while relatively stable during the last few years, currently are 55 percent below the Plan objective.

Most North American ducks breed in Canada and the United States, and winter in the United States and Mexico. For the purposes of this document, North American ducks are divided into three groups based on similarities in ecological requirement: dabbling ducks, diving ducks, and sea ducks.

Status of Dabbling Ducks

Dabbling ducks are the most abundant and widespread group of ducks in North America, and are of greatest importance to sport hunting and viewing. They include the mallard, black duck, mottled duck, American wigeon, northern pintail, gadwall, green-winged teal, blue-winged teal, cinnamon teal, and northern shoveler. The wood duck, muscovy duck, and fulvous and black-bellied whistling ducks, although not true dabbling ducks, also are included in this category (Table 1).

Blue-winged Teal — J.C. Salyer

The highest breeding densities of dabbling duck are found on the prairies. Boreal habitats also support large populations at generally lower densities. Early nesting species, such as mallards and pintails, are particularly affected by losses of upland nesting habitat on the prairies. Intensive agricultural land use on the prairie breeding grounds, combined with drought that began in 1980, adversely affected large segments of breeding habitat into the early 1990s. Habitat degradation and loss, and land-use changes that have favorably affected predator species, continue to hinder waterfowl from achieving historic survival and recruitment rates.

Black Duck — Ducks Unlimited Canada

Six species (mallard, gadwall, American wigeon, green-winged teal, blue-winged teal, and northern shoveler) have exhibited increasing trends in the Mid-continent Region from 1986 to 1998 (Table 2). No trend was evident for Mid-continent northern pintails during the same period.

The black duck population in eastern North America has decreased over the last four decades. Annual winter surveys that were used to index the size of the black duck population estimated an average of 491,000 birds during the 1960s, falling to 285,000 during the 1990s. Although black ducks have declined in both the Atlantic and Mississippi Flyways, the proportional decrease in abundance has been greater in the Mississippi Flyway. Breeding waterfowl surveys initiated in 1990 in eastern Canada indicate that the breeding black duck population has increased in the Maritime Provinces but has shown declines in the western portions of its breeding range. Changes in black duck abundance may be related to habitat losses, competition with mallards, and hunting mortality.

The wood duck occurs primarily in eastern North America, and generally inhabits areas with dense overhead cover. Therefore, estimates of abundance from large-scale aerial surveys typically used to monitor wood duck abundance are not available. Ground-based counts along specified routes, however, suggest both short- and long-term increasing population trends.

Several dabbling duck species occur only in the southern United States and Mexico. Mottled ducks and muscovy ducks are mainly non-migratory. The whistling ducks tend to be nomadic, exhibiting unpredictable movements. Therefore, detecting changes in population status is difficult. While few data currently exist on these populations, information gaps are being addressed.

Black-bellied Whistling-duck — B.J. Rose

Status of Diving Ducks and Sea Ducks

North American diving ducks include the canvasback, redhead, ring-necked duck, greater scaup, and lesser scaup. Although not true diving ducks, ruddy ducks, and masked ducks are included in this category. Highest breeding densities occur on the prairies, although the ring-necked duck and lesser scaup are widespread and the greater scaup breeds mainly in the sub-Arctic. Masked ducks occur primarily in Mexico. Diving ducks tend to use the deeper inland marshes, rivers, and lakes for breeding and migration, and coastal bays, estuaries, and offshore waters for wintering.

Canvasbacks and redheads have exhibited increasing population trends in the Mid-continent Region during recent years (Table 2). The status of individual scaup species (greater and lesser) is difficult to discern, because the two species are difficult to distinguish during aerial surveys. The size of the entire scaup population (primarily composed of lesser scaup), however, has declined since the late 1970s and is the only Mid-continent group that has a decreasing trend since 1986. The continued decline has heightened concerns about these species, prompting public and private management agencies to allocate additional resources to address the problem.

Steller's Eider — Glen Smart

Estimates for breeding populations of ring-necked ducks and ruddy ducks in the Mid-continent Region are not considered as reliable as those for the species in Table 2. Nevertheless, the data suggest that these species have increased in abundance over the long term. No data are available to assess the status of masked ducks.

North American sea ducks include species of the Tribe Mergini, specifically the harlequin duck, oldsquaw, bufflehead, four species of eider, three of scoter, three of goldeneye, and three of merganser. These species breed primarily throughout the northern regions of the continent. Basic biological information is extremely limited for some species, as is a reliable population index or estimate of annual productivity for the 15 species. Spectacled and Steller's eiders in Alaska are listed as threatened. Harlequin ducks in eastern North America have been declared endangered in Canada.

Available data for bufflehead suggest that this species has increased in abundance in surveyed areas over the long term. Goldeneyes have exhibited no apparent trend. The limited abundance data from breeding and wintering areas suggest that mergansers as a group have experienced a long-term increase.

Breeding habitat conditions for most sea duck species have not changed in recent years. Many traditional wintering areas, however, have been degraded by industrial and urban development on both coasts. Effects of the habitat degradation on the populations are unknown, and there are few data on sea duck populations or harvest levels. A summary of available information suggests that some populations are stable or increasing, whereas many may be declining. In November 1998, the formation of a sea duck joint venture was conditionally endorsed to address the management and information needs for these species and to facilitate international coordination and cooperation.

Goose Population Objectives

The Plan establishes population goals for 30 populations of six species of geese. Goose populations occupy traditional breeding and wintering grounds each year, and move between these areas within traditional migration corridors. Consequently, the Plan includes objectives for individual populations of Canada geese, snow geese, white-fronted geese, and brant. Canada, the United States, and Mexico are jointly responsible for the monitoring and management of these populations and species.

Objective
Increase or reduce populations to sustainable levels listed in Table 3

Table 3

Status of and goals for North American goose populations

Species and Population	Population Average (1996–1998)[a]	Recent Trend (1986–1997)[b]	Population Objectives
CANADA GEESE			
Atlantic	50,500	Stable	175,000[c,d]
Atlantic Flyway Resident	968,000	Increasing	550,000[e,f]
North Atlantic	No Estimate	No Estimate	15,000[c]
Southern James Bay	76,000	Stable	100,000[e]
Mississippi Valley	619,600	Stable	900,000[e]
Mississippi Flyway Giants	1,067,000	No Estimate	1,000,000[e]
Eastern Prairie	226,100	Stable	300,000[e]
Western Prairie/Great Plains	446,300	Increasing	285,000[g]
Tallgrass Prairie	292,600	Stable	250,000[g]
Shortgrass Prairie	487,500	Stable	150,000[g]
Hi-Line	169,000	Increasing	80,000[g]
Rocky Mountain	107,000	Stable	60,000[g]
Pacific	8,700	Stable	7,250[c]
Lesser Pacific Flyway	No Estimate	No Estimate	125,000[g]
Dusky	13,700	Stable	Avoid ESA[h] Listing
Cackling	173,000	Increasing	250,000[g]
Aleutian	24,000	Increasing	7,500[g]
Vancouver	No Estimate	No Estimate	Not Yet Established
SNOW GEESE			
Greater	674,000	Increasing	500,000[i]
Mid-continent Lesser	2,742,000	Increasing	1,000,000[g]
Western Central Flyway Lesser	107,900	Increasing	110,000[g]
Wrangel Island Lesser	Not Available[m]	Not Available[m]	120,000[e]
Western Canadian Arctic Lesser	486,000	Increasing	200,000[e]
ROSS GEESE	400,000	Increasing	100,000[e]
WHITE-FRONTED GEESE			
Mid-continent[j]	831,400	Stable	600,000[k]
Tule	5,500[l]	Stable	10,000[g]
Pacific Flyway	313,500	Increasing	300,000[g]
BRANT			
Atlantic	121,800	Stable	124,000[g]
Pacific	141,100	Stable	185,000[g]
EMPEROR GEESE	59,000	Stable	150,000[e]

a Incomplete survey years were excluded from analysis.
b Statistical trend, P≤0.10.
c Breeding pairs objective.
d Objective partitioned: 150,000 pairs Ungava Peninsula; 25,000 pairs boreal Quebec.
e Total breeding population objective.
f Objective partitioned: 450,000 Atlantic Flyway states; 100,000 southern Ontario; based on Atlantic Flyway Spring Waterfowl Plot Survey and CWS-Ontario Spring Ground Survey.
g Winter index objective.
h ESA—Endangered Species Act (United States).
i Spring population index objective; international review of the greater snow goose objective is ongoing.
j Eastern and Western Mid-continent populations have been combined following evaluation of neck collar data.
k Autumn index objective.
l Estimates based on neck collar data.
m A survey is being conducted by the Russian government. Population estimates were not available at time of this document's publication.

Snow geese, Ross' geese, white-fronted geese, emperor geese, brant, and most populations of Canada geese, nest in the northernmost reaches of North America and along the shore of Hudson Bay. Several Arctic nesting goose populations have reached record-high abundances and are considered overabundant. Such large populations can be attributed to high adult survival resulting from the abundance of forage in agricultural habitats on wintering and migratory ranges. Overabundant geese are causing significant damage to croplands, parks, and golf courses. Potentially irreparable damage to Arctic breeding habitats have also occurred as a result of intensive goose foraging. Other Arctic and sub-Arctic nesting goose populations have failed to achieve Plan objectives. The Arctic Goose Joint Venture was established to improve both monitoring and coordinated research of Arctic and sub-Arctic nesting goose populations. This joint venture identifies factors that have contributed to the overabundance of some populations that have limited the recovery of others, and ultimately formulates recommendations for improved management of these populations.

Goose population objectives were developed by joint ventures and flyway councils, in consultation with other groups, based on a number of factors. These include optimal population size for population maintenance, breeding ground carrying capacity, demand for consumptive and non-consumptive human uses, landowner tolerance of crop depredation, and potential for disease outbreaks.

Status of Canada Geese

Nine Canada goose populations currently exceed Plan objectives. Of these, the Atlantic Flyway Resident, Mississippi Flyway Giants, Western Prairie/Great Plains, Hi-Line, and Aleutian populations are still increasing. While no population of Canada geese is in decline, numbers in the Atlantic, Mississippi Valley, Eastern Prairie, and Pacific Populations remain well below Plan population objectives (Table 3). Dusky Canada geese in particular remain a subspecies of special concern. The primary factors limiting these populations are weather, food, and water during breeding and brood-rearing periods, breeding ground predation, and hunting.

Snow Geese flock — Ducks Unlimited Canada

Status of Snow Geese and Ross' Geese

All snow goose populations except the Wrangel Island Population have reached or exceeded Plan objectives, and strategies for checking future growth or reducing populations are under evaluation. Challenges associated with the overpopulation of the Mid-continent Snow Goose Population, which has exceeded Plan objectives by nearly 2 million individuals, and the Greater Snow Goose Population are particularly acute. Consequences of degradation of arctic breeding areas and surrounding landscapes for snow geese and other wildlife are primary concerns. Liberalized harvest of these populations may not be sufficient to stabilize or reverse growth rates. Ross' geese currently exceed Plan objectives by 300 to 900 percent. Therefore, proposals to reduce Ross' Goose Populations also are being considered.

Challenges associated with the overpopulation of the Mid-continent Snow Goose Population … are particularly acute.

Status of White-fronted Geese

White-fronted goose — Glenn O. Chambers

White-fronted geese that migrate through the Central Flyway to winter along the Gulf of Mexico had previously been divided into Eastern and Western Mid-continent Populations. As analysis of neck collar data has demonstrated that Mid-continent white-fronted geese are better described as one unit. An objective (Table 3) is now specified only for the single Mid-continent Population. Since autumn surveys began in 1992, no trend in the Mid-continent Population has been detected. Numbers of Pacific Flyway white-fronted geese are at Plan objectives; however, the Tule population remains low.

Status of Other Geese

Brant populations have recovered since crashing in the 1970s. Currently, the Atlantic Population has exceeded Plan objectives and the Pacific Population has reached approximately 75 percent of Plan goals. The size of both populations is stable. Emperor goose populations are below Plan objectives and population size is stable.

Swan Population Objectives

Plan partners have established objectives for two populations of tundra swans and three populations of trumpeter swans (Table 4). Tundra swan breeding ranges encompass most of the Arctic and sub-Arctic from the west coast of Alaska to the northwest coast of Quebec. The Eastern Population winters primarily in the mid-Atlantic states surrounding the Chesapeake Bay, and the Western Population winters at various locations along the west coast from southern British Columbia to the lower Colorado River in southwest Arizona and California.

Trumpeter swans breed within isolated colonies within a much larger historic breeding range that encompasses the prairies, boreal forests, and Inter-mountain Region from southern Alaska to the western Great Lakes states and Ontario. Population designations of trumpeter swans, which do not make the long annual migrations characteristic of tundra swans, are derived from regions in which they breed and winter.

Objectives

Reach or exceed winter index objectives for eastern and western populations of tundra swans as specified in Table 4

Maintain or exceed recent rates of annual increase in all three populations of trumpeter swans to achieve the autumn index objectives specified in Table 4

Tundra Swan — Ducks Unlimited Canada

Table 4
Status of and goals for North American swan populations

Species and Population	3-Year Winter Population Average (1995–1997)	Recent Trend (1986–1997)	Winter Index Objectives
TUNDRA SWANS			
Eastern Population	82,100	Stable	80,000
Western Population	100,000	Increasing	60,000
TRUMPETER SWANS			
Pacific Coast	16,312[a]	Increasing	43,200[c]
Rocky Mountain	2,600[b]	Increasing	6,800[c]
Interior	1,462[b]	Increasing	2,500[c]

a   1995 index
b   1997 index
c   Autumn index objective

Status of Tundra Swans

The number of tundra swans in the Eastern Population is approximately equal to the Plan population objective. The Western Population is presently nearly twice as large as the population objective specified in the Plan. The former population is stable, while the latter continues to increase.

Status of Trumpeter Swans

Trumpeter swan populations have recovered from critically low numbers in the early 1900s, when some predicted extinction to be imminent. Population objectives presented in Table 4 were developed by projecting present population growth rates out to the year 2015. Consequently, no trumpeter swan population currently approaches Plan objectives. The Rocky Mountain and Pacific Populations are each at approximately 35 percent of objective size. The Interior Population, which is augmented by restoration programs, is at nearly 60 percent of its objective. Plan objectives for Interior trumpeter swans are presently under review by management groups concerned with securing future status while avoiding the overpopulation pitfalls experienced with giant Canada goose re-introductions.

> Trumpeter swan populations have recovered from critically low numbers in the early 1900s, when some predicted extinction to be imminent.

Table 5

North American Waterfowl Management Plan joint venture objectives (acres)

Joint Venture Area	Protection	Restoration	Enhancement
UNITED STATES			
Atlantic Coast	945,000[1]	88,050[1]	121,740[1]
Central Valley Habitat	80,000	120,000	735,000
Gulf Coast	689,000	104,000	958,000
Intermountain West	1,500,000	500,000	500,000
Lower Mississippi Valley	407,000	864,000	1,182,000
Pacific Coast[2]	116,600	21,000[3]	21,000[3]
Playa Lakes	51,000	10,000	25,000
Prairie Pothole	1,891,515	744,898	3,669,500
Rainwater Basin	50,000	30,000[4]	8,333
Upper Mississippi/ Great Lakes Region	1,329,000[1]	605,200[1,3]	605,200[1,3]
U.S. Total	**7,059,115**	**3,087,148**	**7,220,573**
CANADA			
Eastern Habitat	1,435,230	1,221,550[3]	
Pacific Coast[2]	132,400	66,000[3]	
Prairie Habitat	3,600,000[5]	3,600,000[3]	
CANADIAN TOTAL	**5,167,630**	**4,887,550[3]**	
MEXICO	To be determined		
PLAN TOTAL	**12,226,745**	**5,530,923**	**9,664,348**

1 Objectives currently under revision.
2 International joint venture.
3 Habitat improvement objectives do not distinguish between restoration and enhancement. For this table, such acres are assumed to represent restoration and enhancement at a 1:1 ratio.
4 Includes 24,000 acres restoration and 6,000 acres of habitat creation.
5 Habitat objective is to secure and improve prairie habitat, both wetlands (760,000 acres) and uplands (2,840,000 acres).

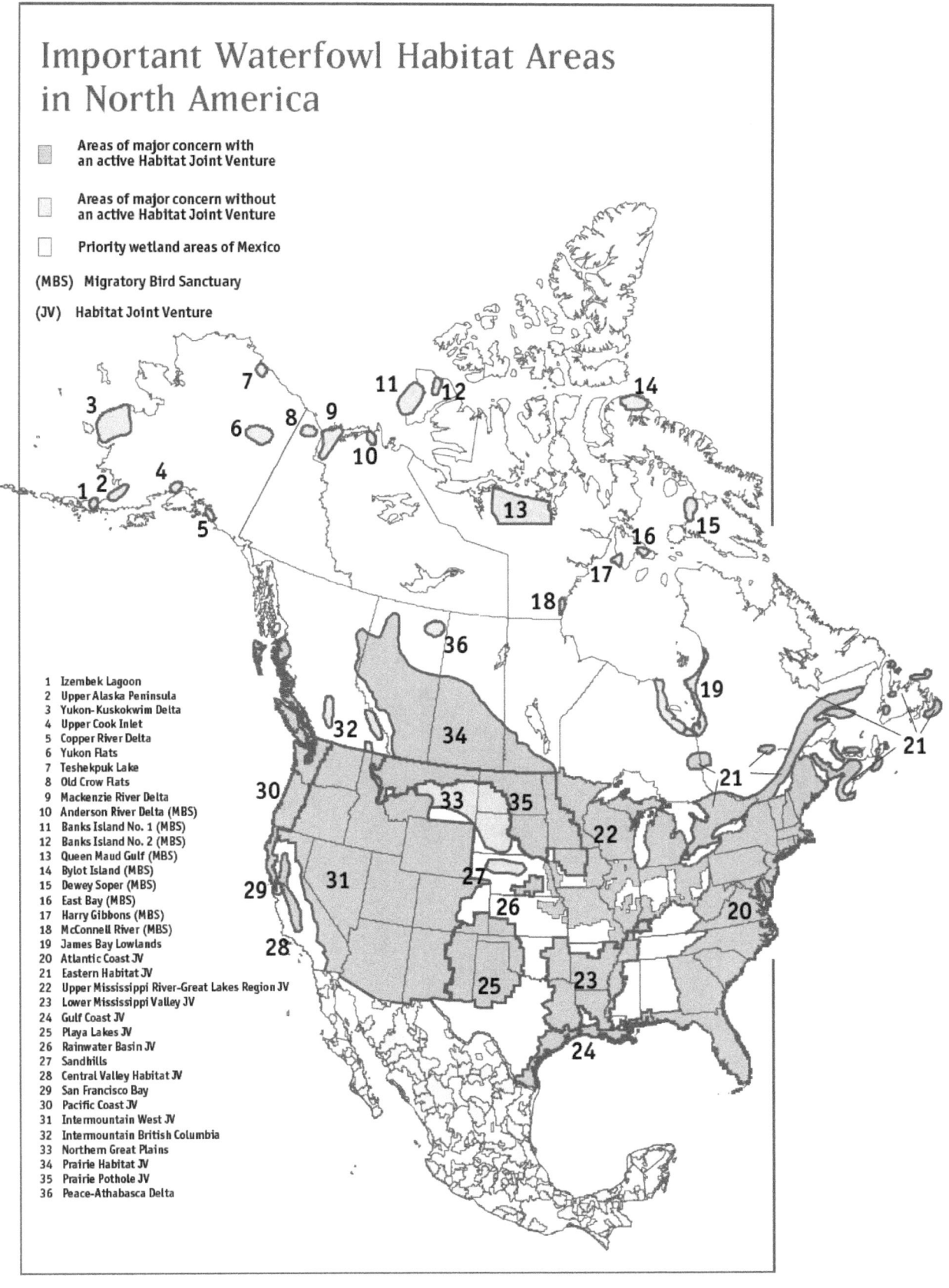

Important Waterfowl Habitat Areas in North America

- Areas of major concern with an active Habitat Joint Venture
- Areas of major concern without an active Habitat Joint Venture
- Priority wetland areas of Mexico

(MBS) Migratory Bird Sanctuary

(JV) Habitat Joint Venture

1 Izembek Lagoon
2 Upper Alaska Peninsula
3 Yukon-Kuskokwim Delta
4 Upper Cook Inlet
5 Copper River Delta
6 Yukon Flats
7 Teshekpuk Lake
8 Old Crow Flats
9 Mackenzie River Delta
10 Anderson River Delta (MBS)
11 Banks Island No. 1 (MBS)
12 Banks Island No. 2 (MBS)
13 Queen Maud Gulf (MBS)
14 Bylot Island (MBS)
15 Dewey Soper (MBS)
16 East Bay (MBS)
17 Harry Gibbons (MBS)
18 McConnell River (MBS)
19 James Bay Lowlands
20 Atlantic Coast JV
21 Eastern Habitat JV
22 Upper Mississippi River-Great Lakes Region JV
23 Lower Mississippi Valley JV
24 Gulf Coast JV
25 Playa Lakes JV
26 Rainwater Basin JV
27 Sandhills
28 Central Valley Habitat JV
29 San Francisco Bay
30 Pacific Coast JV
31 Intermountain West JV
32 Intermountain British Columbia
33 Northern Great Plains
34 Prairie Habitat JV
35 Prairie Pothole JV
36 Peace-Athabasca Delta

PART 3

North American Waterfowl Management Plan Administration

International Administration

North American Waterfowl Management Plan Committee

The North American Waterfowl Management Plan Committee consists of 18 members, 6 from each country, selected from agencies responsible for waterfowl management in Canada, the United States, and Mexico. Members are appointed by the director of the national wildlife agency in the respective country to carry out the following duties.

- Serve as a forum for discussing major, long-term international waterfowl issues and problems, and translate those discussions into recommendations for consideration by the cooperating countries.
- Update the Plan approximately every 5 years in response to new or changing circumstances, policy development, or opportunities.
- Approve new joint ventures/regional partnerships or other partner structures, and review and approve their implementation and evaluation plans to ensure they further the Plan's purpose.
- Facilitate, advise, and maintain close links and communication with joint ventures/ regional partnerships, other Plan delivery mechanisms, and Plan partners on implementation of the Plan.
- Review and monitor progress toward achieving the Plan's population goals and habitat objectives.
- Review scientific and technical data on the status and dynamics of waterfowl populations and their habitats as they relate to the objectives of the Plan.

- Establish and encourage linkages with other international migratory bird, wildlife, and/or habitat initiatives.
- Establish and encourage linkages with appropriate national and international organizations or agencies to ensure that waterfowl conservation is integrated into sustainable use of landscapes.
- Provide a forum for international communication.
- Consider and, if needed, recommend additional actions to the federal governments of Canada, the United States, and Mexico. The Plan Committee directs all recommendations through the Canadian Wildlife Service, the U.S. Fish and Wildlife Service, and the National Institute of Ecology in Mexico.

Continental Evaluation Team

The Continental Evaluation Team was established by the Plan Committee to develop, coordinate, and conduct biological evaluation of the performance of the Plan. Its responsibilities include refining the Plan evaluation strategy; coordinating habitat monitoring efforts; advising joint ventures/regional partnerships in the integration of monitoring and evaluation programs; coordinating and conducting broad-scale evaluations; and summarizing and reporting evaluation progress and implications.

The North American Wetlands Conservation Council

The North American Wetlands Conservation Act of 1989 established the North American Wetlands Conservation Council to review the merits of wetlands conservation proposals submitted for funding under the Act's grants program. The Council ranks and prioritizes projects based on certain biological criteria and recommendations made by joint venture management boards in the United States and by the Canadian and Mexican federal governments. The Council recommends proposals for funding to the Migratory Bird Conservation Commission, the funding authority under the Act.

National Administration

The national coordinating offices for the Plan provide strategic, staff, financial, administrative, and logistical support for the activities of the Plan Committee, the Continental Evaluation Team, and Plan joint ventures/regional partnerships.

Canada

In Canada, the Plan is administered by the North American Wetlands Conservation Council (NAWCC) (Canada). Working with its counterpart in the United States and the National Institute of Ecology in Mexico, the NAWCC (Canada) advises the Minister of the Environment on the development, coordination, and implementation of wetland conservation initiatives of national or international importance.

National coordination is provided by the North American Waterfowl Management Plan Implementation Office, Canadian Wildlife Service, Environment Canada, and the Secretariat of NAWCC (Canada). These offices provide funding support; maintain an accomplishment tracking system; publish the Plan's newsletter, *Waterfowl 2000* (in cooperation with the United States and Mexico); publish the Plan Contact List; and coordinate with joint ventures and the provinces to achieve Plan goals in Canada.

Joint venture management boards and the provincial steering committees have formed many partnerships. Canadian partners include the federal government, all the provincial governments, and numerous government agencies, conservation organizations, municipalities, corporations, and landowners. These partners are directly responsible for designing, implementing, and monitoring programs and projects across the country.

United States

In the United States, the Plan has become a network led by the joint ventures to connect diverse programs aimed at migratory bird and habitat conservation on public and private lands.

Public-lands management is directed at acquiring high-priority public lands and restoring, enhancing, and managing habitats on existing lands. Partners include all of the states that participate in a joint venture and most of the major federal land-management agencies, such as the U.S. Fish and Wildlife Service's National Wildlife Refuge System, the National Park Service, the Bureau of Land Management, the Bureau of Reclamation, the Bureau of Indian Affairs, the Department of Agriculture Forest Service, and the Department of Defense.

Private-lands management is directed at improving wetland, grassland, and forest habitats for waterfowl. Private lands are conserved through a diverse network of programs and partnerships, including the U.S. Fish and Wildlife Service's Partners for Fish and Wildlife, corporate partnerships, private-lands programs conducted by conservation organizations, and federal programs such as the Department of Agriculture's Wetlands Reserve Program, the Conservation Reserve Program, and the Environmental Quality Improvement Program.

National coordination is provided by the Service's North American Waterfowl and Wetlands Office. It provides funding support; maintains an accomplishment tracking system; conducts national evaluation activities; publishes the Plan's newsletter, *Waterfowl 2000* (in cooperation with Canada and Mexico), annual progress reports, and other reports; and coordinates with other federal agencies and the U.S. Congress.

Mexico

In Mexico, conservation under the Plan is coordinated through the National Institute of Ecology. Conservation efforts are directed at improving the overall conditions of wetland ecosystems within a framework of the great wealth of Mexico's biological diversity. The economic importance of waterfowl is relatively small in Mexico, and is dwarfed by the economic and social importance of all aspects of biological resources. Conservation projects are developed, implemented, and managed in cooperation with local communities. Conservation education is an integral part of conservation delivery. Developing sustainable uses of wetlands and other habitats, and working with local communities to develop and implement management plans, is a high priority.

Regional partnerships have developed in key wetland areas in Mexico, and work is underway to further develop inventory information and databases, develop additional species and habitat conservation projects, and refine priorities.

Regional Administration

Joint Ventures

Joint venture management boards provide strategic oversight and guidance to ensure that Plan goals are being achieved. Boards review feedback from evaluation programs and maintain an updated implementation strategy that reflects current understanding of the joint venture efforts needed to support Plan continental population objectives. Management boards identify the most effective conservation techniques (intensive programs, extensive programs, policy influence) and the relative importance of each in meeting joint venture landscape objectives. They also develop and secure funding for conservation projects. In addition to habitat-focused joint ventures, species joint ventures have also been formed to address monitoring and research needs of specific species or species groups. The species joint ventures are international in scope as well.

Habitat Joint Ventures

Atlantic Coast Joint Venture
Central Valley Habitat Joint Venture
Eastern Habitat Joint Venture
Gulf Coast Joint Venture
Intermountain West Joint Venture
Lower Mississippi Valley Joint Venture
Pacific Coast Joint Venture (United States and Canada)
Playa Lakes Joint Venture
Prairie Habitat Joint Venture
Prairie Pothole Joint Venture
Rainwater Basin Joint Venture
Upper Mississippi River – Great Lakes Region Joint Venture

Additional habitat joint ventures are expected to develop over time in many of the remaining waterfowl areas of major concern. For example, the Plan Committee looks forward to approving a San Francisco Bay Joint Venture in 1999. In Mexico, regional partnerships exist in many parts of the nation to accomplish the Plan's goals.

Species Joint Ventures

Arctic Goose Joint Venture (United States and Canada)
Black Duck Joint Venture (United States and Canada)

The Plan Committee encourages additional partnerships wherever there are significant gaps in data necessary to conserve waterfowl and when financial support and interests from partners exist. Such efforts should be part of, or closely coordinated with, habitat joint ventures. Of note, the Plan Committee looks forward to approving a Sea Duck Joint Venture in 1999.

Over 50% recycled paper
including 20% post
consumer fibre

M An official mark of Environment Canada

Cover photo: Pintail — David Stimac, David Stimac Photography

Ce document est aussi disponible en français sous le titre
Plan nord amercain de gestion de la sauvagine
Mise à jour de 1998, Une vision élargie

Este documento esta disponible en español con el título
Plan de Manejo de Aves Acuáticas de Norteamérica
Actualización de 1998, Ampliando la visión

 U.S. Department of the Interior,
Fish and Wildlife Service

 Environment   Environnement
Canada   Canada

Canadian Wildlife   Service canadien
Service   de la faune

 SEMARNAP
SEMARNAP   Mexico
MÉXICO

Printed in Canada 05/99

 Biological Foundation

 Landscape Approach

 Partnerships

  Canada   U.S.A.   Mexico

NAWMP Implementation Office
Wildlife Conservation Branch
Canadian Wildlife Service
Environment Canada
Place Vincent Massey, 3rd Floor
351 St. Joseph Boulevard
Hull, Québec
Canada   K1A 0H3

Phone: (819) 997-2392
Fax: (819) 994-4445
E-mail: nawmp@ec.gc.ca

North American Waterfowl
and Wetlands Office
U.S. Fish and Wildlife Service
Arlington Square Building
4401 North Fairfax Drive, Room 110
Arlington, Virginia
U.S.A. 22203

Phone: (703) 358-1784
Fax: (703) 358-2282
E-mail: r9arw_nawwo@mail.fws.gov

Instituto Nacional de Ecología - SEMARNAP
Dirección General de Vida Silvestre
Avenida Revolución /1425, nivel 19
Colonia Tlacopac, San Angel
México, D.F.
México   01040

Phone: +(52-5) 624-3301
Fax: +(52-5) 624-3588